WHAT IS TIME?

Contents

Written by Simon Mugford

Collins

What is time?

Have you ever wondered *what time is?*
It can mean different things; it just depends on how you think about it!

We experience time as the way everything – *that's all the stuff in the universe* – moves along from the past, to the present and on into the future.

Time is also the *gap* between two or more different events. Think about an ordinary Monday morning – you leave for school and then you arrive at school. The gap between you leaving home and arriving at school is the *time* it takes to get there.

Can you stop time?

Time itself keeps going and it can't be stopped. Time was moving before you put your coat on to go to school and it kept going after you sat down at your desk. Time keeps on going, wherever you are and whatever you're doing!

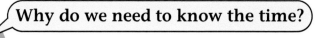

Why do we need to know the time?

Imagine a world where nobody knew what the time was. There would be no timetables, so you wouldn't know when to catch a bus or a train. You wouldn't know when school started or finished, or when shops opened or closed. It would be chaos!

We need to know the time so that we can plan our lives. We use it to arrange to see our friends and family, to go to work and school – and to have fun.

How do you tell the time?

Time is measured by clocks and watches. They can tell us the time more accurately than just morning or afternoon, night or day. There are 24 hours in a day, so a clock shows the same time twice a day.

How does a clock tell the time?

A clock is divided up into 12 hours. Each hour has 60 minutes.

"O'clock" is the time when the big hand points to 12.

The big hand points to the minute.

The little hand points to the hour.

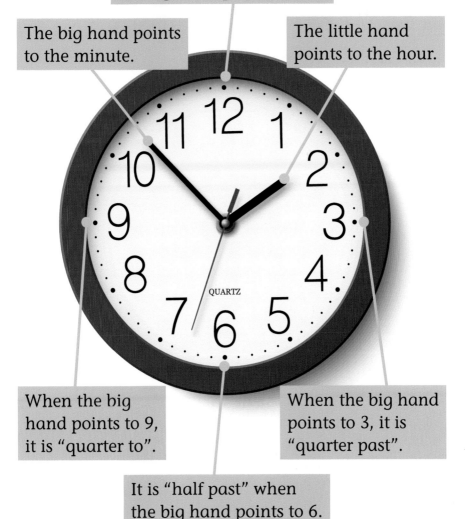

When the big hand points to 9, it is "quarter to".

When the big hand points to 3, it is "quarter past".

It is "half past" when the big hand points to 6.

How does a clock work?

The first types of clock were mechanical. A mechanical clock uses springs, weights and gears that move at a regular time. Mechanical clocks need to be wound up to work.

The gears are connected to the hands, which show the time on the clock face.

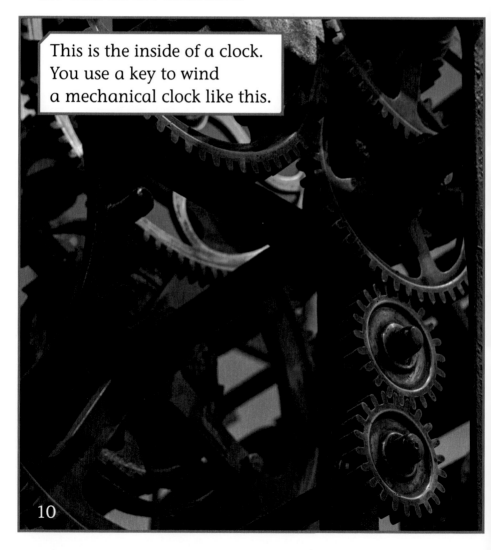

This is the inside of a clock. You use a key to wind a mechanical clock like this.

When were clocks invented?

Mechanical clocks first appeared in the 14th century, often on towers of important buildings.

The clock on the town hall in Florence, Italy, was built in 1353. It only has one hand!

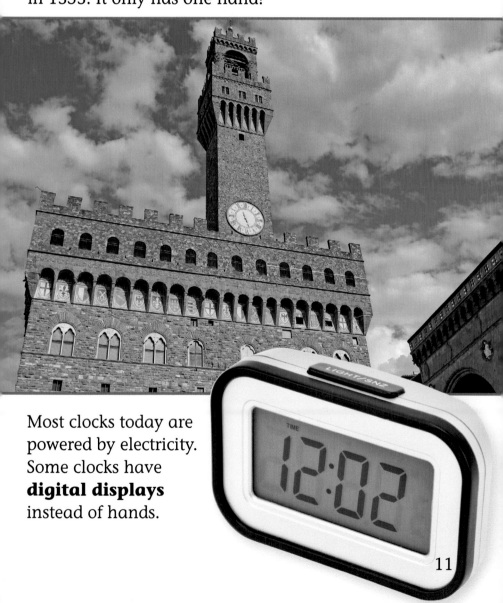

Most clocks today are powered by electricity. Some clocks have **digital displays** instead of hands.

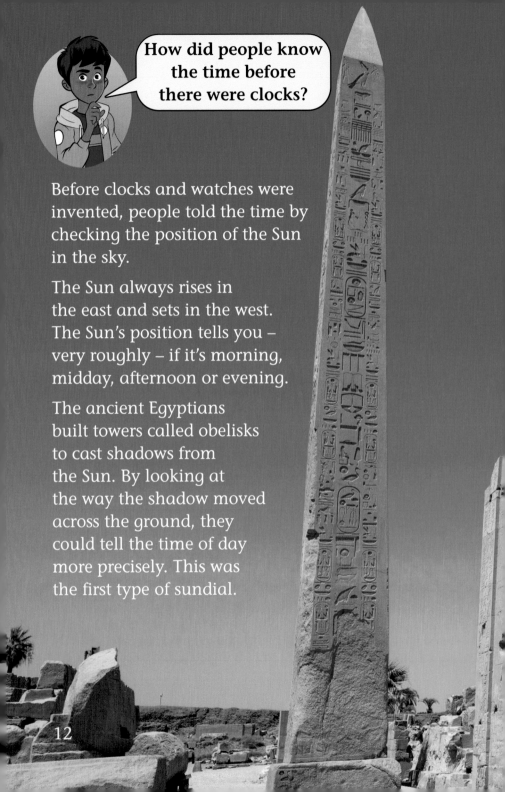

How did people know the time before there were clocks?

Before clocks and watches were invented, people told the time by checking the position of the Sun in the sky.

The Sun always rises in the east and sets in the west. The Sun's position tells you – very roughly – if it's morning, midday, afternoon or evening.

The ancient Egyptians built towers called obelisks to cast shadows from the Sun. By looking at the way the shadow moved across the ground, they could tell the time of day more precisely. This was the first type of sundial.

Later, sundials had a numbered face with a pointer, called a gnomon.

Why are there 24 hours in a day?

A day is the length of time it takes the earth to make one complete turn on its axis. The axis is an invisible line running through the middle of the earth, between the North and South Poles.

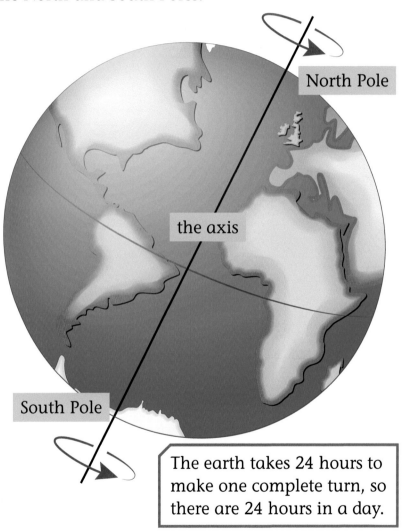

North Pole

the axis

South Pole

The earth takes 24 hours to make one complete turn, so there are 24 hours in a day.

Why do we have night and day?

As the earth **rotates**, one side faces towards the Sun and the other side faces away from it. It is daytime on the light side and night-time on the dark side of the earth.

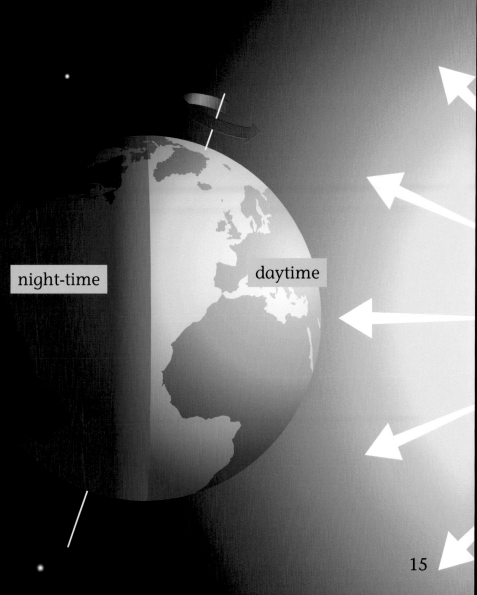

night-time

daytime

15

Why are there 365 days in a year?

The earth spins on its axis each *day*, but it's also travelling around (orbiting) the Sun. It takes about 365 days – one year – to make one full orbit of the Sun.

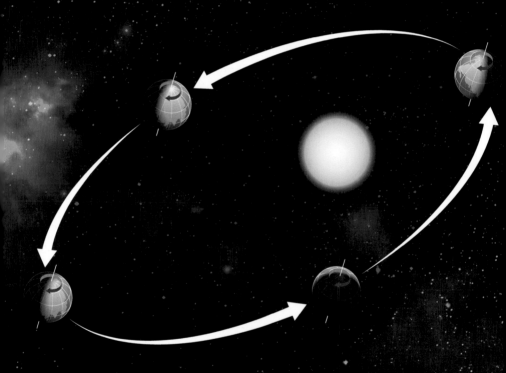

Why do we have seasons?

The earth is slightly **tilted** on its axis, so as it orbits the Sun, one half of the planet has more sunlight than the other. This changes as the earth orbits, causing the seasons.

The **Northern Hemisphere** has more sunlight from June to August.

The **Southern Hemisphere** has more sunlight from December to February.

Is it the same time everywhere in the world?

When it's night-time on one side of the world, it will be daytime on the other side, so it can't be the same time of day everywhere. Time zones divide the world up, so that each time zone has its own time.

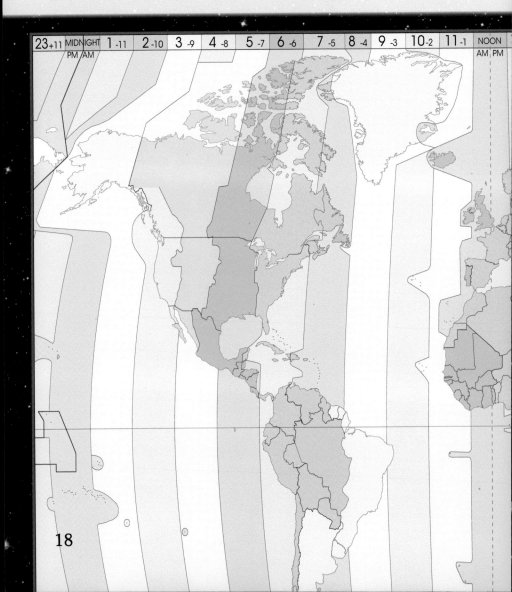

23 +11	MIDNIGHT	1 -11	2 -10	3 -9	4 -8	5 -7	6 -6	7 -5	8 -4	9 -3	10 -2	11 -1	NOON
	PM / AM												AM / PM

Can I travel in time?

Yes, sort of! As you move from one time zone to another, the time of day changes by one hour. The International Date Line is an imaginary line on the earth that separates each day.

2	15+3	16+4	17+5	18+6	19+7	20+8	21+9	22+10	23+11	MIDNIGHT	1 -11	2 -10	3 -9	4 -8
										PM \ AM				

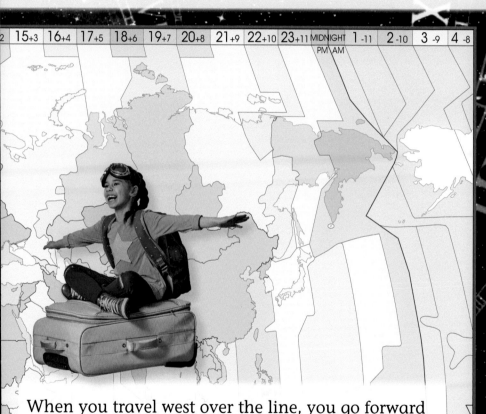

When you travel west over the line, you go forward a day. Go east and you travel back to the day before!

But so far, no one has invented a time travel machine to take them anywhere in time!

Is time the same on other planets?

Each planet in our solar system spins on its axis and orbits the Sun at different speeds. This means that the lengths of days and years on other planets are different from those on Earth.

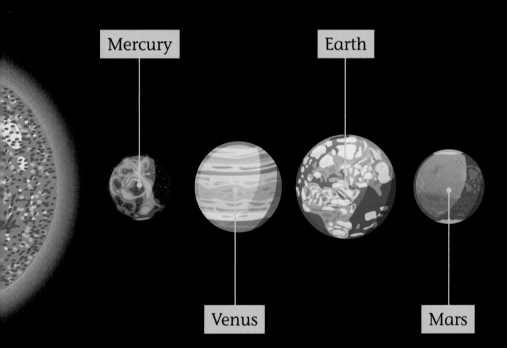

Venus takes 243 Earth days to spin on its axis and 224.7 Earth days to orbit the Sun.

So, a day on Venus is longer than a year on Earth!

If you're six years old now, you would be nearly 25 on Mercury, but you would be six months old on Jupiter!

Jupiter

Uranus

Saturn

Neptune

Why do some months have more days than others?

The movements of the earth, Sun and Moon that we use to measure time are not **exact**. A solar year (one orbit of the Sun) is actually $365\frac{1}{4}$ days.

Months are based on the time it takes the Moon to orbit the earth. A lunar (moon) month is $29\frac{1}{2}$ days.

To make 12 lunar months fit neatly into a solar year, 11 extra days are added to the year, spread out across the months.

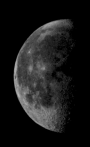

What is a leap year?

Every four years, an extra day is added to the month of February to help keep the calendar correct.
When February has 29 days instead of 28 days, this is called a leap year.

Does everyone in the world use the same calendar?

The calendar used by most countries and people in the world is the Gregorian calendar, created by a pope called Gregory in 1582.

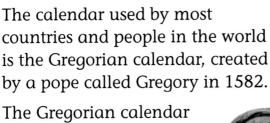

The Gregorian calendar is a version of the Julian calendar, which was created by the Roman Emperor Julius Caesar.

Many countries and religions around the world use lunar calendars, based on moon cycles, for the dates of festivals and celebrations. These dates change each year.

Muslims celebrate Eid at different times each year.

A dragon costume is worn to celebrate Chinese New Year, which is celebrated between 21st January and 21st February.

Where do the names for the months come from?

The months of the year were named by the ancient Romans, when Julius Caesar created the Julian calendar.

Caesar named the month of July after himself!

August is named after another Roman emperor, Augustus.

March is named after Mars, the Roman god of war. It was originally the first month of the Julian calendar.

June takes its name from the goddess Juno.

September, October, November and December are named after the **Latin** words for seven, eight, nine and ten.

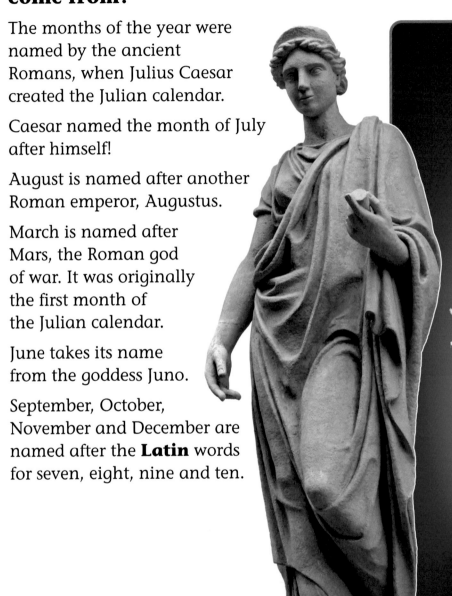

The movement of time is always there, taking you through the months, the days and the years.

Glossary

digital displays information (in this case, time) given in the form of numbers

exact something that is absolutely right

Latin language spoken in ancient Rome

Northern Hemisphere the half of the earth that is north of the equator (an invisible line that divides the earth into two)

rotates turns on a central point

Southern Hemisphere the half of the earth that is south of the equator (an invisible line that divides the earth into two)

tilted in a sloping position

Index

Time ...

... to play with friends

... to celebrate

... to go to bed

... to time travel?

Ideas for reading

Written by Christine Whitney
Primary Literacy Consultant

Reading objectives:
- retrieve information from non-fiction
- be introduced to non-fiction books that are structured in different ways
- explain and discuss their understanding of books

Spoken language objectives:
- ask relevant questions
- speculate, imagine and explore ideas through talk
- participate in discussions

Curriculum links: History: Develop an awareness of the past, use common words and phrases relating to the passing of time; Writing: Write for different purposes

Word count: 1359

Interest words: calendar, seasons, axis, lunar, orbit, tilted

Build a context for reading
- Ask children what they understand by the word *time*. What time did they get up today? How long does it take them to get to school? What is the time now?
- Read the title of the book and ask children what they expect to read about in this book.
- Challenge children to ask three questions about *time*. Check for answers when reading the book.

Understand and apply reading strategies
- Read up to page 6 together and ask children to explain to each other why we need to know the time.
- Continue to read and pause at page 17. Ask children to explain to each other why we have seasons using the words: *seasons, axis, orbit* and *tilted*.
- How long is a *solar year*? How long is a *lunar month*? What is a *leap year*? Children should work in pairs to find the answer to these questions.
- Ask children to explain the use of the contents page. Suggest that they ask each other for the page number where they might find the answer to this question: *When were clocks invented?*